JUMP!

GAZELLES

Lynette Robbins

PowerKiDS
press
New York

For Sue Lynette, my mom

Published in 2012 by The Rosen Publishing Group, Inc.
29 East 21st Street, New York, NY 10010

First Edition

Editor: Joanne Randolph
Book Design: Ashley Drago and Erica Clendening

Photo Credits: Cover Nigel Dennis/Getty Images; p. 4 © www.iStockphoto.com/Johan Swanepoel; p. 5 Digital Vision/Thinkstock; pp. 6–7 David Madison/Getty Images; p. 8 © www.iStockphoto.com/Rick Wylie; p. 9 (top) © www.iStockphoto.com/André van der Veen; p. 9 (bottom) Ken Lucas/Getty Images; pp. 10–11 Gerald Hinde/Getty Images; pp. 12–13, 15, 18, 20 Shutterstock.com; pp. 14, 17 Tom Brakefield/Stockbyte/Thinkstock; pp. 16, 22 Paul Souders/Getty Images; p. 19 © www.iStockphoto.com/Peter ten Broecke; p. 21 iStockphoto/Thinkstock.

Library of Congress Cataloging-in-Publication Data

Robbins, Lynette.
 Gazelles / by Lynette Robbins. — 1st ed.
    p. cm. — (Jump!)
 Includes index.
 ISBN 978-1-4488-5014-3 (library binding) — ISBN 978-1-4488-5161-4 (pbk.) —
 ISBN 978-1-4488-5162-1 (6-pack)
 1. Gazelles—Juvenile literature. I. Title.
 QL737.U53R57 2012
 599.64'69—dc22

                                    2011000344

Manufactured in the United States of America

CPSIA Compliance Information: Batch #WS11PK: For Further Information contact Rosen Publishing, New York, New York at 1-800-237-9932

Contents

Good Morning, Gazelle!

It is morning on the African **savanna**. A herd of gazelles has gathered in the early morning light. Some of the gazelles are **grazing** on dewy grass. The fawns, or babies, are playing together and learning how to jump. The males, or bucks, are listening for **predators** to help keep the herd safe.

Gazelles, such as this springbok, have ringed horns. They have stripes and other markings on their fur, too.

Suddenly, a buck jumps high into the air. The herd gets the message. A predator is nearby! As a cheetah dashes from the brush, the gazelles are already running and jumping to get away. This time they are lucky. The cheetah moves off in search of other **prey**.

Gazelles can jump high and far when necessary. Springbok like these can jump 11 feet (3 m) high and as far as 49 feet (15 m) in one bound.

Gazelles at Home

Gazelles live in Africa and in southwest and central Asia. Most gazelles live on dry, grassy plains and savannas where it is very warm. Some live on cold plains, called **steppes**. All gazelles like open spaces.

Some kinds of gazelles live in the desert. These gazelles can live in very hot weather. They do not need much water to live. The rhim gazelle lives in

the Sahara desert. Its coat is a light color to **reflect** the sunlight.

Some gazelles can live where it is very cold. Tibetan gazelles live in high mountain meadows. They grow thick fur in the winter to help keep them warm.

Here Thomson's gazelles and Grevy's zebras graze together in the Masai Mara National Reserve, in Kenya. The Masai Mara is mostly open grassland.

7

Kinds of Gazelles

A gazelle is a kind of small to medium-sized antelope. There are 16 different **species** of gazelles. The most common species are Thomson's gazelles and Grant's gazelles. These two kinds of gazelles often graze together. Gazelles have long, slender necks and legs. They have long, ringed horns. Some kinds of gazelles have curved horns. Other kinds of gazelles have straight horns.

Thomson's gazelles can run as fast as 40 miles per hour (64 km/h). They live in East Africa. Males have thick, ringed horns. Females, though, have very thin horns or none at all.

The dama gazelle is the largest species of gazelle. A dama gazelle can weigh 190 pounds (85 kg). The smallest gazelle is the Dorcas gazelle. A Dorcas gazelle is likely smaller than you! It weighs only about 44 pounds (20 kg).

BELOW: Dama gazelles are endangered, or in danger of disappearing from Earth. There are only a few hundred dama gazelles left.

ABOVE: Springbok live in South Africa, Namibia, and Botswana. Male springbok are larger than the females and have thicker horns.

Those Amazing Jumpers

Gazelles can jump high into the air. A gazelle jumps by lifting all four of its feet into the air at once. It bends its back and holds its legs straight out. This kind of jumping is called **stotting**. Some biologists think that one reason that gazelles stot is to try to fool their predators.

Predators often hunt weak or sick animals. A gazelle may stot to show that it is strong and healthy. The predator that sees a gazelle stotting might decide that it cannot catch such a strong animal. It may look for easier prey. Stotting also may confuse the predator and give gazelles a moment to get away. Stotting could also help tell other gazelles that danger is near.

Scientists have many guesses as to why gazelles stot. One of their ideas is that gazelles may stot when they are trying to find a mate.

Gazelle Facts

1 Although male gazelles use their horns to fight each other, they almost never hurt each other. Their ringed horns lock together while they are fighting.

5 Bucks protect the herd by listening and looking for predators. Bucks are also the first to go near a water hole. They make sure it is safe for the rest of the herd.

6 Rhim gazelles live in the Sahara desert. They have extra wide hooves. Their wide hooves help them walk on the sand.

7 A Speke's gazelle has folds of skin around its nose that it can inflate to make a honking sound. The sound is used to tell other gazelles when danger is nearby.

Predators will eat nearly half of all Thomson's gazelle fawns before they grow into adults.

2

People overhunted the Arabian and Yemen gazelles, and now they are **extinct**.

3

A long time ago, the Egyptians and the Romans **domesticated** the Dorcas gazelle. Dorcas gazelles were raised on farms and used to feed many people.

4

8

In most gazelle species, both the males and females have horns.

9

Gazelles in zoos can live for up to 17 years. They have shorter life spans in the wild.

13

Grazing Gazelles

Gazelles are **herbivores.** This means they eat only plants. Gazelles eat grass, leaves, shoots, and sometimes fruit. Gazelles do not need to drink much water. They get almost all the water they need from the plants that they eat.

Gazelles sometimes stand on their back legs to reach leaves from high branches. They use their front hooves to help keep their balance.

Many gazelles eat different things in different seasons. They like young, green grasses best in the wet season. Some gazelles will dig up wild melons and cucumbers for their water in the dry season.

Just like cows and sheep, gazelles have stomachs with four parts. When a gazelle chews and swallows its food, it goes into the first stomach. Then wads of food are forced up from the stomach back into the gazelle's mouth and chewed again. When it is swallowed the second time, the food goes through the other three parts of the gazelle's stomach.

15

Fast Getaway!

Gazelles have many predators. Lions, leopards, cheetahs, hyenas, and wolves all hunt gazelles. Most gazelles live on open plains, where there is nowhere to hide. Instead they must be fast to escape their predators.

A gazelle can run up to 50 miles per hour (80 km/h) for up to 20 minutes! That is fast, but it may not be fast

Cheetahs are one of gazelles' many enemies. If a gazelle does not get a head start, it could be hard for it to outrun a cheetah, which can run 70 miles per hour (113 km/h).

enough to outrun a cheetah or a pack of hyenas. That is why a gazelle may try to trick or surprise its predator by suddenly jumping into the air. If the gazelle is lucky, it will get away. If it is not, its death helps other animals live.

Once a predator is spotted, the whole herd starts to run. The fastest and strongest live on to graze another day. The slowest animals become food for a hungry hunter.

Life in a Herd

Gazelles live in herds. Herds can be made up of as few as 5 animals or as many as 200. Gazelles spend most of their time grazing. They may share their **territories** with other grazing animals, such as antelopes and zebras. During the day, the herd may spread out. In the evenings, though, the members of the herd all come back together.

Gazelle herds are generally made up of all males or all females and their young. The size and makeup of different herds is always changing, though.

Some herds **migrate.** Gazelles that live in the mountains migrate to lower, warmer places in the winter. They move to places where there is more to eat. In places where there is a dry season and a rainy season, herds of gazelles may travel more than 100 miles (160 km) to find water.

Huge herds of gazelles, zebras, and wildebeests migrate each year across the Serengeti Plain to the Masai Mara Reserve to find food and water.

Fighting and Fawns

During the **mating** season, the male gazelles leave the herd. Males set up territories. A male will fight other males that enter his territory. Males fight with their horns. When a herd of females enters a male's territory, the male may mate with several of them.

Female gazelles give birth to one fawn at a time. The fawn spends the first few

Thomson's gazelles can give birth twice a year. The mother carries the baby for about six months before it is born. She then cares for her young until it joins the herd.

weeks of its life hiding in the tall grass or bushes. The mother returns to the fawn several times a day to nurse. When the fawn is strong enough to run fast, it joins the herd. A female gazelle can start mating at around one year old.

Male gazelles fight by butting their horns together. They do not stab with their horns, though, so the losers are not generally hurt. They just leave with headaches!

Gazelles in Danger

Some species of gazelles are endangered. This means they are in danger of becoming extinct. Some of these include the Cuvier's gazelle, the dama gazelle, and the rhim gazelle. One reason gazelles are endangered is because people have hunted too many of them. People hunt gazelles for their meat, hide, and horns. Another reason these gazelles are endangered is because people have destroyed their grazing lands to build farms, factories, and cities.

Gazelles are important animals. They help keep the grasslands where they live healthy when they eat the plants. They also feed many animals that share their habitat.

In some places, endangered species of gazelles are protected. It is against the law to hunt gazelles in these places. If gazelles have enough protected places to live, someday they may not be endangered!

Glossary

domesticated (duh-MES-tih-kayt-id) Raised to live with people.

extinct (ik-STINGKT) No longer existing.

grazing (GRAYZ-ing) Feeding on grass.

herbivores (ER-buh-vorz) Animals that eat only plants.

mating (MAYT-ing) Coming together to make babies.

migrate (MY-grayt) To move from one place to another.

predators (PREH-duh-terz) Animals that kill other animals for food.

prey (PRAY) An animal that is hunted by another animal for food.

reflect (rih-FLEKT) To throw back light, heat, or sound.

savanna (suh-VA-nuh) A grassland with few trees or bushes.

species (SPEE-sheez) One kind of living thing. All people are one species.

steppes (STEPS) Treeless lands with few plants, found in very cold places.

stotting (STOT-ing) Jumping straight up.

territories (TER-uh-tor-eez) Land or space that animals guard for their use.

Index

B

babies, 4

brush, 5

buck(s), 4–5, 12

C

cheetah(s), 5, 16–17

D

desert, 6–7, 12

G

grass, 4, 14, 21

H

herd(s), 4–5, 12, 18–21

P

plains, 6, 16

predator(s), 4–5, 10–13, 16–17

S

savanna(s), 4, 6

season, 19–20

species, 8–9, 13, 22

steppes, 6

stotting, 10–11

T

territories, 18, 20

Web Sites

Due to the changing nature of Internet links, PowerKids Press has developed an online list of Web sites related to the subject of this book. This site is updated regularly. Please use this link to access the list:
www.powerkidslinks.com/jump/gazelles/